TRINITY
COLLEGE LONDON PRESS

GRADE

03
BASS

Published by
Trinity College London Press Ltd.
trinitycollege.com

Registered in England
Company no. 09726123

Photography by Zute Lightfoot, lightfootphoto.com

Printed in England by Caligraving Ltd.

Parental and Teacher Guidance:

The songs in Trinity's Rock & Pop syllabus have been arranged
to represent the artists' original recordings as closely and
authentically as possible. Popular music frequently deals with
subject matter that some may find offensive or challenging.
It is possible that the songs may include material that some
might find unsuitable for use with younger learners.

We recommend that parents and teachers exercise their own
judgement to satisfy themselves that the lyrics of selected
songs are appropriate for the students concerned. As you
will be aware, there is no requirement that all songs in this
syllabus must be learned. Trinity does not associate itself with,
adopt or endorse any of the opinions or views expressed in
the selected songs.

THE EXAM AT A GLANCE

In your exam you will perform a set of three songs and one of the session skills assessments. You can choose the order of your set list.

SONG 1

Choose a song from this book.

SONG 2

Choose *either* a different song from this book
or a song from the list of additional Trinity Rock & Pop arrangements, available at trinityrock.com
or a song you have chosen yourself: this could be your own cover version or a song that you have written. It should be at the same level as the songs in this book and match the parameters at trinityrock.com

SONG 3: TECHNICAL FOCUS

Song 3 is designed to help you develop specific and relevant techniques in performance. Choose one of the technical focus songs from this book, which cover two specific technical elements.

SESSION SKILLS

Choose *either* **playback** *or* **improvising**.

Session skills are an essential part of every Rock & Pop exam. They are designed to help you develop the techniques music industry performers need.

Sample tests are available in our *Session Skills* books and free examples can be downloaded from trinityrock.com

ACCESS ALL AREAS

GET THE FULL ROCK & POP EXPERIENCE ONLINE AT TRINITYROCK.COM

We have created a range of digital resources to support your learning and give you insider information from the music industry, available online. You will find support, advice and digital content on:

- Songs, performance and technique

- Session skills

- The music industry

You can access tips and tricks from industry professionals featuring:

- Bite-sized videos that include tips from professional musicians on techniques used in the songs

- 'Producer's notes' on the tracks, to increase your knowledge of rock and pop

- Blog posts on performance tips, musical styles, developing technique and advice from the music industry

JOIN US ONLINE AT:

 /TRINITYROCKANDPOP    @TRINITY_ROCK    /TRINITYROCKANDPOP   and at **TRINITYROCK.COM**

CONTENTS

(I'M A) ROAD RUNNER   5   TECHNICAL FOCUS

ANOTHER ONE BITES THE DUST   9

COME TOGETHER   13

MISERY BUSINESS   17   TECHNICAL FOCUS

PAPA'S GOT A BRAND NEW BAG   23

SEASONS (WAITING ON YOU)   27   TECHNICAL FOCUS

SONG 2   31

WALKING ON THE MOON   35

HELP PAGES   38

THE AUDIO

Professional demo & backing
tracks can be downloaded free,
see inside cover for details.

Music preparation and book layout by Andrew Skirrow for Camden Music Services
Music consultants: Nick Crispin, Chris Walters, Christopher Hussey, Mike Mansbridge
Audio arranged, recorded & produced by Tom Fleming
Bass arrangements by Sam Burgess & Ben Heartland

Musicians
Bass: Ben Heartland
Drums: George Double
Guitar: Tom Fleming
Sax: Derek Nash
Vocals: Bo Walton, Alison Symons, Brendan Reilly

YOUR
PAGE
NOTES

TECHNICAL FOCUS

(I'M A) ROAD RUNNER

JR WALKER & THE ALLSTARS

WORDS AND MUSIC: BRIAN HOLLAND, LAMONT DOZIER, EDDIE HOLLAND

SINGLE BY
Jr Walker & The Allstars

ALBUM
Road Runner

B-SIDE
Shoot Your Shot

RELEASED
1966

RECORDED
1965
Hitsville U.S.A.
Detroit, Michigan, USA

LABEL
Tamla Motown

WRITERS
Brian Holland
Lamont Dozier
Eddie Holland

PRODUCER(S)
Brian Holland
Lamont Dozier

Arkansas-born saxophonist Autry DeWalt II formed his first instrumental group, Jumping Jacks, in his teens. He was nicknamed Junior by his stepfather, whose name was Walker. Signing to Motown in 1964, he became the label's prime exponent of raw, hard-driving R&B.

Featuring Junior Walker on lead vocals and tenor sax, '(I'm a) Road Runner' was written and produced by the legendary Holland-Dozier-Holland, the Motown hitmakers behind 25 US No. 1 hits by the likes of The Supremes, Four Tops and Marvin Gaye. When they came to produce the record, the trio discovered that Walker could only play the sax part in two keys, so they had him sing in one key and play the sax in another. The saxophone track was then sped up to match the vocal which, combined with the baritone sax and guitar parts, helped give the whole recording an urgent, punchy sound. James Jamerson of Motown's in-house band The Funk Brothers played bass on the session, and his inventive playing can be heard on countless other classics from the label. The song first appeared on Walker's 1965 debut album *Shotgun* and was released as a single in 1966, reaching No. 20 in the US and No. 12 in the UK three years later.

TECHNICAL FOCUS

Two technical elements are featured in this song:

- Syncopation
- Articulation

Syncopation appears mainly in the intro. Aim for precision here, and play melodically, which will provide contrast with the repeated notes that make up the next section. **Articulation** is important throughout – especially in accented notes at end of the intro (and where this material returns) and in the verse. Here, the tenuto markings suggest a full-length, slightly emphasised note, while the brackets suggest an underemphasised or 'ghosted' note.

TECHNICAL FOCUS

(I'M A) ROAD RUNNER

WORDS AND MUSIC:
BRIAN HOLLAND, LAMONT DOZIER, EDDIE HOLLAND

Intro

'60s Soul ♩ = 128 (1½ bars count-in)

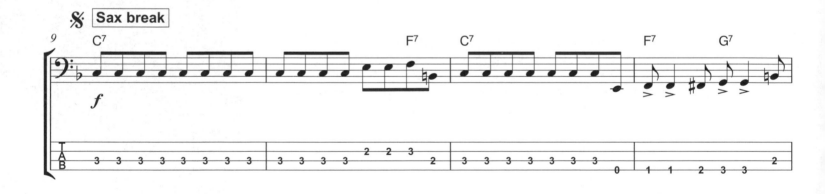

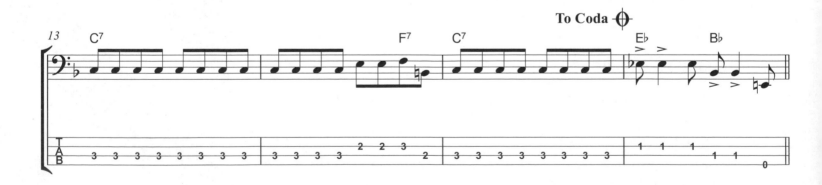

YOUR
PAGE
NOTES

ANOTHER ONE BITES THE DUST QUEEN

WORDS AND MUSIC: JOHN DEACON

SINGLE BY
Queen

ALBUM
The Game

B-SIDE
Dragon Attack

RELEASED
1980

RECORDED
**June-July 1979 &
February-May 1980
Musicland Studios
Munich, Germany**

LABEL
EMI

WRITER
John Deacon

PRODUCERS
**Queen
Mack**

Queen formed in London, England in 1970, with an early output that straddled hard rock, prog rock and heavy metal. All four members provided material, and with each successive album they honed their sound to embrace inventive yet polished and radio-friendly pop to immense global success.

'Another One Bites the Dust' was the fourth single to be released from Queen's eighth album, 1980's *The Game*. It became their second song to top the US singles chart following 'Crazy Little Thing Called Love' from the same album. Credited to the band's bassist John Deacon, the taut, funky, groove-based song marked a notable departure from their familiar rock sound. Michael Jackson, a fan of Queen's, suggested it be released as a single, although drummer Roger Taylor was initially against the idea. It went on to become a huge hit, even beating 'Bohemian Rhapsody' to remain the band's biggest-selling single and notching up sales of over seven million copies worldwide.

⚡ PERFORMANCE TIPS

This song is a simple classic, built from a short riff that appears in the bass part throughout. Your job is to play this riff stylishly and consistently, with a strong detached feel on the staccato crotchets. A similar but new riff comes in at the verse – here you'll need a high level of rhythmic precision.

ANOTHER ONE BITES THE DUST

WORDS AND MUSIC: JOHN DEACON

Intro

Rock ♩ = 110 (2 bars count-in)

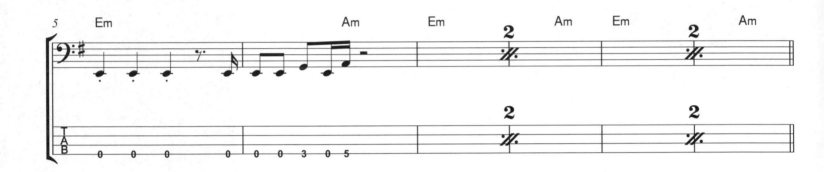

Verse

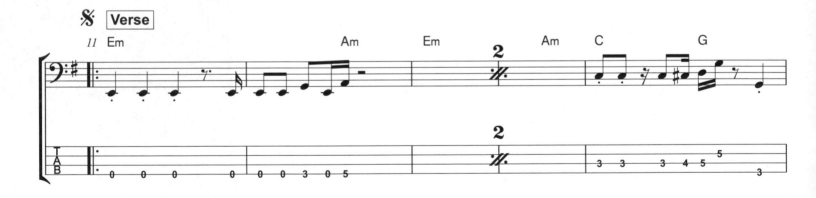

YOUR
PAGE
NOTES

COME TOGETHER
THE BEATLES

WORDS AND MUSIC: JOHN LENNON, PAUL MCCARTNEY

SINGLE BY
The Beatles

ALBUM
Abbey Road

B-SIDE
Something

RELEASED
**26 September 1969
(album)
31 October 1969
(single)**

RECORDED
**21-30 July 1969
EMI Studios
London, England**

LABEL
Apple

WRITERS
**John Lennon
Paul McCartney**

PRODUCER
George Martin

With skills honed at Liverpool's Cavern Club, The Beatles emerged in the early 60s as a tight-knit rock'n'roll band with a flourishing songwriting duo in frontmen John Lennon and Paul McCartney. Signed to EMI in 1962 by producer George Martin, band and producer would together create a succession of records in a whirlwind of creativity spanning just eight years, changing the face of music.

'Come Together' came about after American psychologist, author and LSD champion Timothy Leary asked Lennon to write him a campaign song for his planned run against Ronald Reagan for the governorship of California in 1969 (Leary coining the phrase 'Come together, join the party' as his campaign slogan). Although neither campaign nor theme song worked out, the request ultimately inspired one of The Beatles' greatest final recordings. The opening track of the band's last album to be recorded, 1969's *Abbey Road*, it was released as a double A-side with George Harrison's 'Something' as the album's only single. It became The Beatles' 18th No. 1 in America, their eventual total of 20 still the most by any one act. Lennon later said of 'Come Together' that 'it was a funky record – it's one of my favourite Beatles tracks.'

⚡ PERFORMANCE TIPS

The opening of this song must be one of the most iconic riffs in rock'n'roll, so it's worth taking some time to achieve the authentic sound! The written-in slides will help you get there, as will observing the quaver rest. Take care over the grace notes in bar 18. Bar 21 requires repeated quavers that are rhythmically even but with changing articulations (short-long-short-long etc).

COME TOGETHER

WORDS AND MUSIC:
JOHN LENNON, PAUL MCCARTNEY

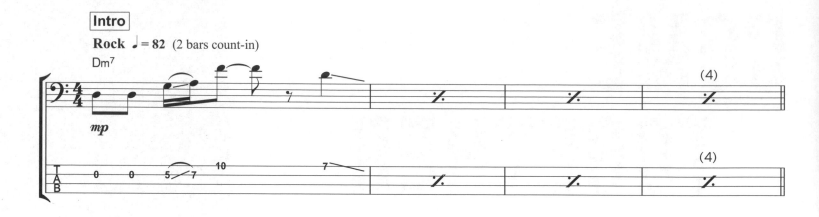

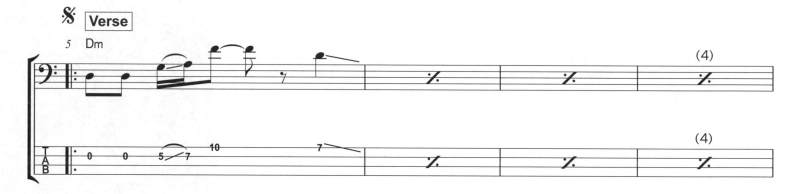

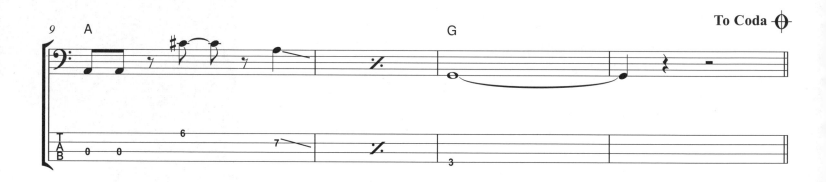

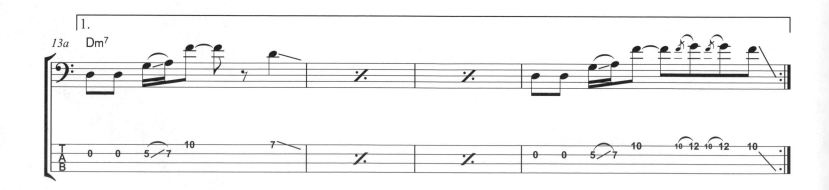

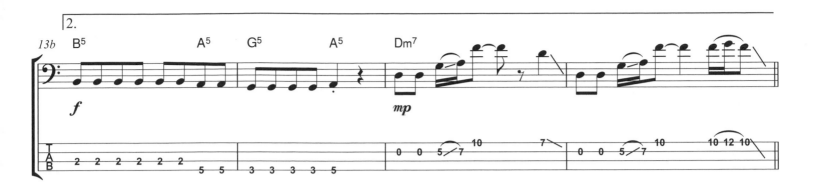

Instrumental

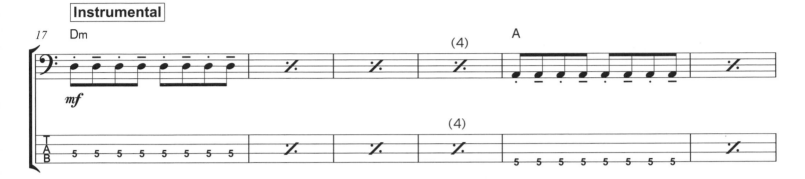

D.S. al Coda

Coda

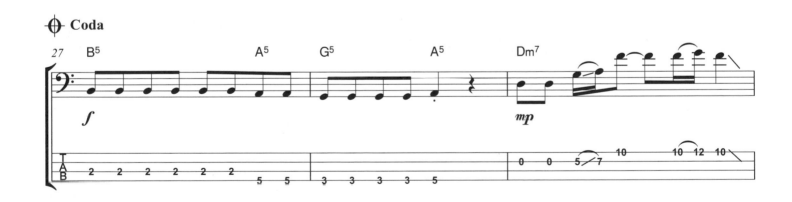

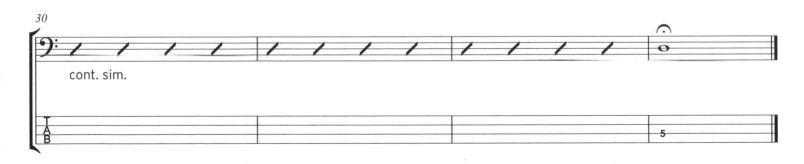

YOUR
PAGE
NOTES

SINGLE BY
Paramore

ALBUM
Riot!

B-SIDE
**Stop this Song
(Love Sick Melody)**

RELEASED
4 June 2007

RECORDED
**January-March 2007
House Of Loud, Elmwood
Park, New Jersey, USA
(album)**

LABEL
Fueled by Ramen

WRITERS
**Hayley Williams
Josh Farro**

PRODUCER
David Bendeth

TECHNICAL FOCUS

MISERY BUSINESS
PARAMORE

WORDS AND MUSIC: HAYLEY WILLIAMS, JOSH FARRO

Please note: This song contains subject matter that some might find inappropriate for younger learners. Please refer to the Parental and Teacher Guidance at the beginning of this book for more information.

Paramore were formed in Tennessee in 2004 by Hayley Williams (vocals), Jeremy Davis (bass) and brothers Josh and Zac Farro (guitar and drums respectively). The band have released four albums since 2005, their commercial breakthrough coming with 2007's *Riot!*

'Misery Business' was released as the lead single from *Riot!*, reaching No. 17 in the UK and No. 26 in the US (eventually going on to sell over three million copies in their homeland alone). Williams wrote the lyrics when she was 17 years old, based on real events she experienced in high school. The origins of the song concerned the singer enough to post a message on the band's social media page, asking fans to post what they are ashamed of. She later said:

> I found that people really were reaching out to someone to spill their guts to, so I did the same thing lyrically in the song and let everything out. It's more honest than anything I've ever written, and the guys matched that emotion musically.

The ear-catching intro, made to sound like an old sample, is performed by the Mexican band Mariachi Real de Mexico.

TECHNICAL FOCUS

Two technical elements are featured in this song:

- Palm muting while using the pick
- Articulation

The beginning of the song requires **palm muting while using the pick**, at a soft dynamic. This will require careful control of the picking hand, and you'll also need to bring out the accents in bar 4. **Articulation** requires precision throughout, but take particular care at bars 37–44 where there are both staccato and accented quavers.

TECHNICAL FOCUS

MISERY BUSINESS

WORDS AND MUSIC:

HAYLEY WILLIAMS, JOSH FARROPAPA

Intro

Rock ♩ = 173 (2 bars count-in)

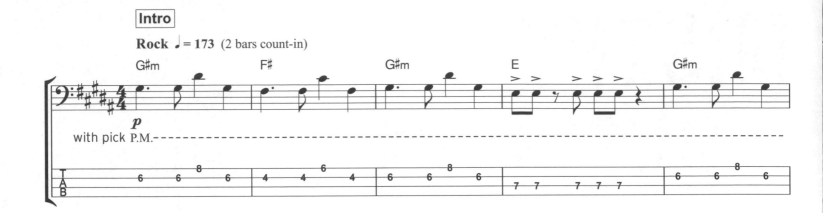

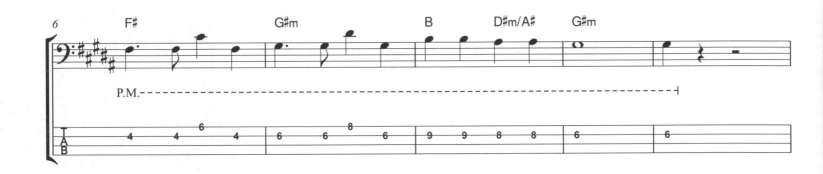

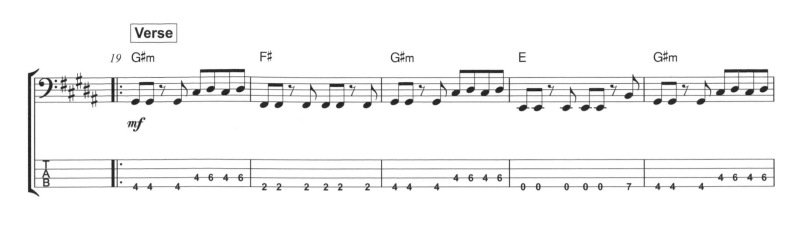

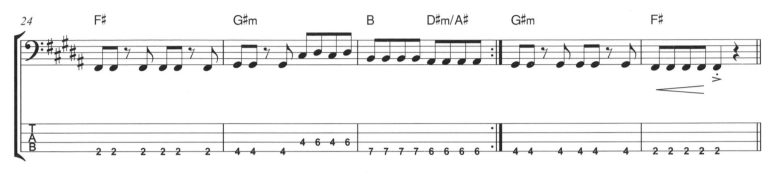

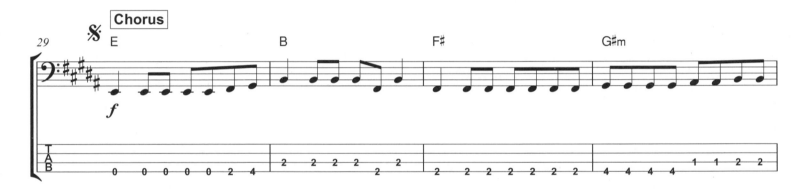

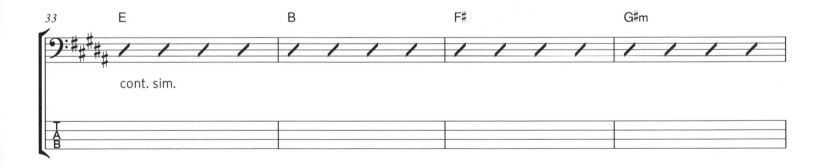

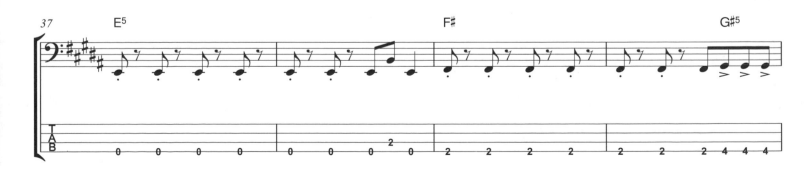

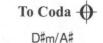

Breakdown

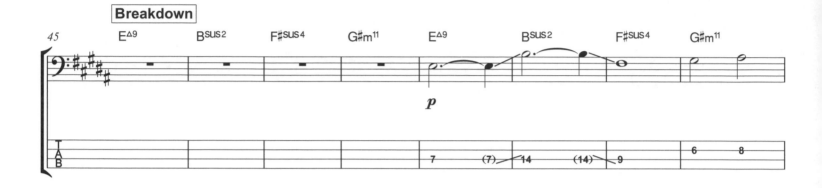

Instrumental

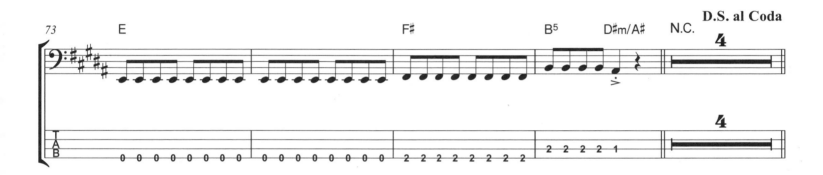

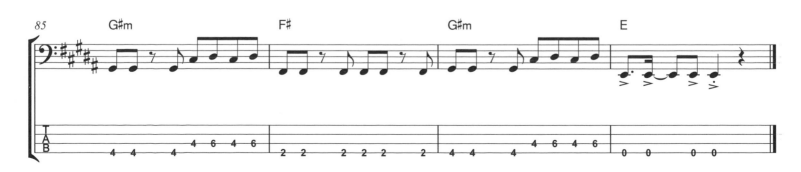

YOUR
PAGE
NOTES

PAPA'S GOT A BRAND NEW BAG JAMES BROWN

WORDS AND MUSIC: JAMES BROWN

SINGLE BY
James Brown

ALBUM
Papa's Got a Brand New Bag

B-SIDE
Papa's Got a Brand New Bag Part II

RELEASED
June 1965

RECORDED
1 February 1965 Arthur Smith Studios Charlotte, North Carolina, USA

LABEL
King

WRITER
James Brown

PRODUCER
James Brown

Often referred to as The Godfather of Soul, South Carolina-born James Brown started as a gospel singer before making his writing and recording debut in 1956 with the R&B hit 'Please, Please, Please'. One of the most influential and dynamic artists in music history, he combined rhythm and blues with elements of jazz and gospel alongside innovations that came to be known as funk.

1965's 'Papa's Got a Brand New Bag' was a stylistic statement of intent for James Brown as he moved away from soulful ballads to a rawer, more arresting new sound first suggested by the previous year's rhythmically pioneering 'Out of Sight'. Starting out as a vamp at their live shows, Brown and his band The Famous Flames dropped into a studio in North Carolina on their way to a concert and laid down the song in one take. Brown recalled:

> We stopped to listen to the playback to see what we needed to do on the next take. While we were listening, I looked around the studio. Everybody – the band, the studio people, me – was dancing. Nobody was standing still. Later on they said it was the beginning of funk.

Almost seven minutes long, the recording was edited for single release and sped up for greater impact. It became Brown's first top-ten US hit and first UK hit.

⚡ PERFORMANCE TIPS

The tenuto lines in this song indicate a half accent – less than an accent but clearly marking the downbeat. In the words of Bootsy Collins, James Brown's bass player: 'Mr Brown wanted me to just keep it simple and keep on hitting that "one".' So, aim for consistency and drive, and enjoy the bass feature moments like those at bars 7 and 10.

PAPA'S GOT A BRAND NEW BAG

WORDS AND MUSIC: JAMES BROWN

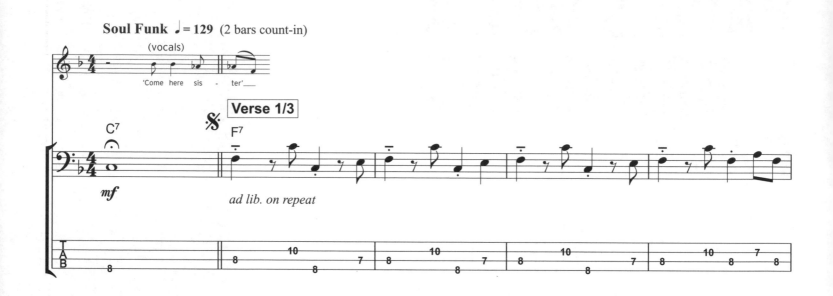

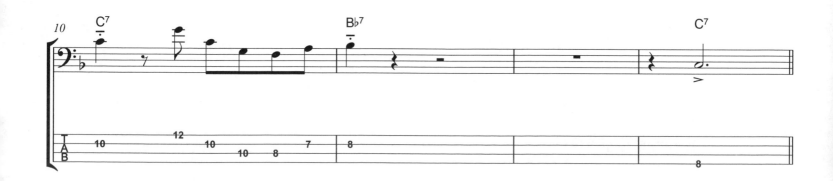

Verse 2/4

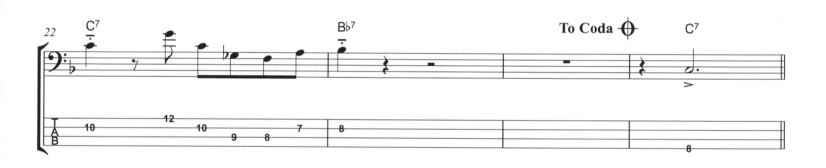

Bridge

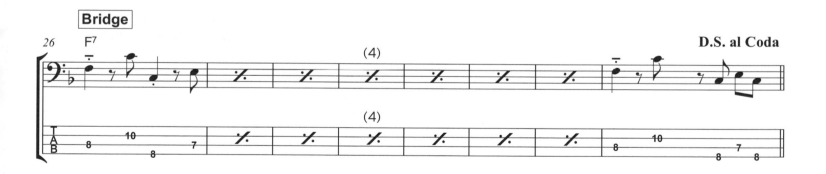

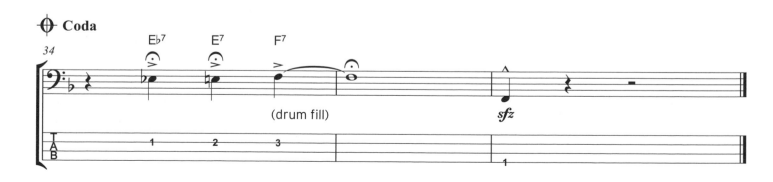

YOUR
PAGE
NOTES

TECHNICAL FOCUS

SEASONS (WAITING ON YOU) FUTURE ISLANDS

**WORDS AND MUSIC: WILLIAM CASHION, SAMUEL T HERRING
GERRIT WELMERS**

SINGLE BY
Future Islands

ALBUM
Singles

B-SIDE
One Day

RELEASED
4 February 2014

RECORDED
**August 2013
Dreamland Studios
Hurley, New York, USA**

LABEL
4AD

WRITERS
**William Cashion
Samuel T Herring
Gerrit Welmers**

PRODUCER
Chris Coady

The three members of Future Islands met at university in North Carolina and released their debut album in 2006. Featuring Samuel T Herring (vocals), Gerrit Welmers (keyboards/programming) and William Cashion (bass/guitars), the band found international success with the release of their fourth album, 2014's *Singles*.

Before the release of 'Seasons (Waiting on You)', Future Islands were a little-known, cult act. The event that really changed the band's fortunes overnight occurred on 3 March 2014, when they made their network television debut on *The Late Show with David Letterman*, performing the song live. Herring's intense delivery and show-stealing moves elicited an effusive reaction from the host and viewing audience, before becoming a viral hit around the world after the clip was posted on YouTube. Eight years after forming, the band found themselves to be overnight sensations, suddenly being offered high-profile TV spots and festival slots around the world. By the end of 2014, 'Seasons' had been voted the top song of the year by *NME*, *Spin*, *The Village Voice*, *Time Out*, *Pitchfork* and *Consequence of Sound*.

TECHNICAL FOCUS

Two technical elements are featured in this song:

- Syncopation
- Slides

The bass part of this song uses a lot of repeated quavers, sometimes with added ties to create **syncopation**. Keep the quavers steady and make the syncopation rhythmically consistent every time it appears. The bridge and the outro use **slides** to move between pitches – this is a flamboyant effect that can be emphasised.

TECHNICAL FOCUS

SEASONS (WAITING ON YOU)

WORDS AND MUSIC: WILLIAM CASHION, SAMUEL T HERRING, GERRIT WELMERS

'Cause I've been waitin' on you.

SONG 2
BLUR

**WORDS AND MUSIC: DAMON ALBARN, GRAHAM COXON
ALEX JAMES, DAVE ROWNTREE**

03 GRADE
BASS

SINGLE BY
Blur

ALBUM
Blur

B-SIDE
**Get Out of Cities
Polished Stone
Bustin' + Dronin'
Country Sad Ballad Man
(live acoustic)**

RELEASED
**10 February 1997 (album)
7 April 1997 (single)**

RECORDED
June-November 1996

**Stúdíó Grettisgat,
Reykjavik, Iceland**

**Maison Rouge Studio
Studio 13, & Mayfair
Studios, London, England**

LABEL
Food / Parlophone

WRITERS
**Damon Albarn
Graham Coxon
Alex James
Dave Rowntree**

PRODUCER
Stephen Street

Formed in London, England in the late-80s, Damon Albarn (vocals/keyboards), Graham Coxon (guitar/vocals), Alex James (bass) and Dave Rowntree (drums) became one of the UK's biggest bands of the 90s, six of their eight studio albums reaching No. 1.

1997's self-titled fifth album saw Blur dramatically shift from the chirpy Britpop of their previous three albums – *Modern Life Is Rubbish* (1993), *Parklife* (1994) and *The Great Escape* (1995) – to embrace a rawer and more lo-fi sound influenced by leftfield American bands such as Pavement and Sonic Youth. Describing the making of the song, Alex James told Q Magazine: 'It was kind of a throwback. We'd always done brainless rocking out, though maybe it's not what we're known for.' As well as reaching No. 2 in the UK the song became the band's breakthrough hit in the US. The celebratory sounding 'woo hoo!' of the chorus has also seen the song adopted by sports teams from around the world when marking goals, touchdowns, home runs and game wins.

⚡ PERFORMANCE TIPS

There is some fast picking to negotiate in this song as well as some rapid position changes, for example at the ends of bars 24 and 34. Distortion is used in places to create a heavy rock effect. Playing in this heavy rock style requires 'letting go' a bit, but you'll also need to keep a tight grip on the musical detail – a delicate balancing act!

SONG 2

WORDS AND MUSIC:
DAMON ALBARN, GRAHAM COXON,
ALEX JAMES, DAVE ROWNTREE

Intro

Heavy Indie Rock ♩ = 116 (2 bars count-in)

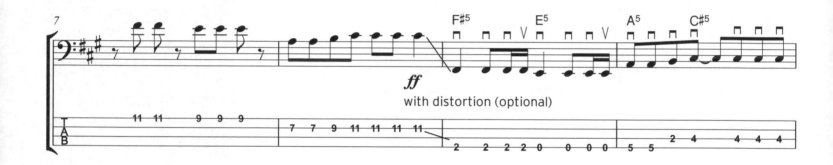

Verse

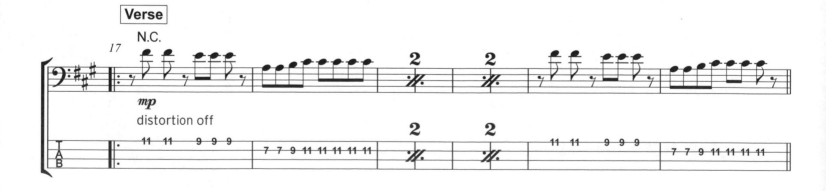

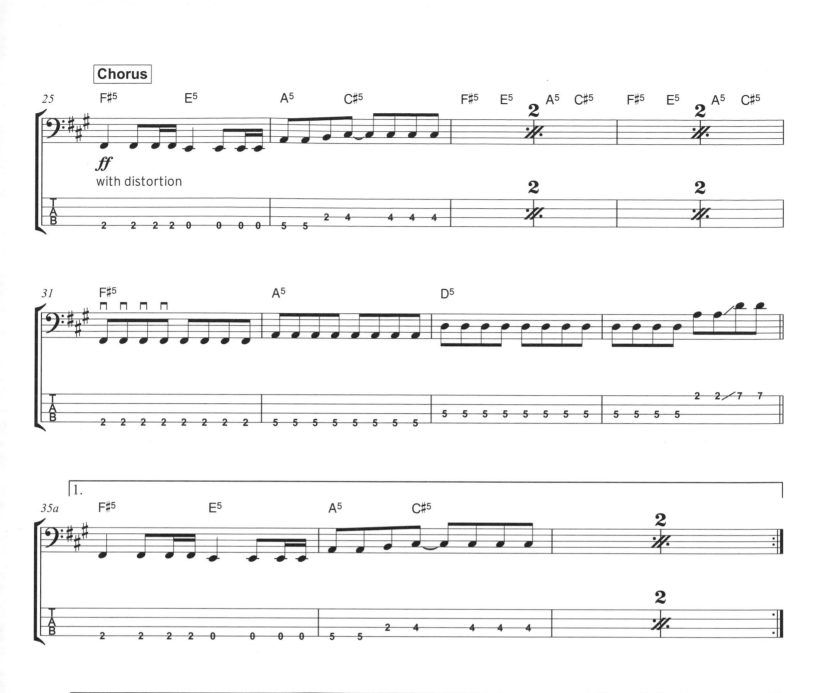

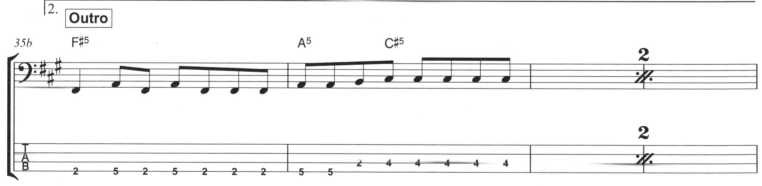

YOUR
PAGE
NOTES

WALKING ON THE MOON

THE POLICE

WORDS AND MUSIC: STING

SINGLE BY
The Police

ALBUM
Reggatta de Blanc

B-SIDE
Visions of the Night

RELEASED
4 November 1979

RECORDED
**1979
Surrey Sound Studios
Leatherhead
Surrey, England**

LABEL
A&M

WRITER
Sting

PRODUCERS
**Nigel Gray
The Police**

Formed in London, England in 1977 by songwriter Sting (vocals, bass), Andy Summers (guitar) and Stewart Copeland (drums), The Police were together for less than a decade but became one of the world's best-selling groups over the course of five studio albums. The band split at their peak, following their biggest album *Synchronicity* and the UK/US No. 1 hit 'Every Breath You Take'.

The Police's second No. 1, 'Walking on the Moon', followed hot on the heels of their first, 'Message in a Bottle', just eight weeks separating them. Both songs were taken from the band's second album, *Regatta de Blanc*, the first of six No. 1 albums for the group. According to Sting, he woke with the tune in his head and improvised the lyrics as he walked around a Munich hotel room. He commented: 'Walking on the moon seemed a useful metaphor for being in love, that feeling of lightness, of being able to walk on air.' In 2000 he reflected: 'If you've got the right riff, the song can just write itself. That's what happened with "Walking on the Moon". I wish I could find another one of those every day: a simple, easy, three-note or four-note riff. The whole song is based around its cadence, and I'm very proud of that.'

⚡ PERFORMANCE TIPS

As Sting himself commented, this song is all about the opening riff — listen to the original to capture the right amount of separation between the notes. Later, in the bridge, there are some syncopated repeated notes that will require precision. At bars 51–60 you have the opportunity to ad lib on this material before returning to the notated part at bar 41.

WALKING ON THE MOON

WORDS AND MUSIC: *STING*

CHOOSING SONGS FOR YOUR EXAM

SONG 1

Choose a song from this book.

SONG 2

Choose a song which is:

Either a different song from this book

or from the list of additional Trinity Rock & Pop arrangements, available at trinityrock.com

or from a printed or online source

or your own arrangement

or a song that you have written yourself

You can play Song 2 unaccompanied or with a backing track (minus the bass part). If you like, you can create a backing track yourself (or with friends), add your own vocals, or be accompanied live by another musician.

The level of difficulty and length of the song should be similar to the songs in this book and match the parameters available at trinityrock.com

When choosing a song, think about:

- Does it work on my instrument?

- Are there any technical elements that are too difficult for me? (If so, perhaps save it for when you do the next grade)

- Do I enjoy playing it?

- Does it work with my other songs to create a good set list?

SONG 3: TECHNICAL FOCUS

Song 3 is designed to help you develop specific and relevant techniques in performance. Choose one of the technical focus songs from this book, which cover two specific technical elements.

SHEET MUSIC

If your choice for Song 2 is not from this book, you must provide the examiner with a photocopy. The title, writers of the song and your name should be on the sheet music. You must also bring an original copy of the book, or a download version with proof of purchase, for each song that you perform in the exam.

Your music can be:

- A lead sheet with lyrics, chords and melody line

- A chord chart with lyrics

- A full score using conventional staff notation

PLAYING WITH BACKING TRACKS

All your backing tracks can be downloaded from soundwise.co.uk

- The backing tracks begin with a click track, which sets the tempo and helps you start accurately

- Be careful to balance the volume of the backing track against your instrument

- Listen carefully to the backing track to ensure that you are playing in time

If you are creating your own backing track, here are some further tips:

- Make sure that the sound quality is of a good standard

- Think carefully about the instruments/sounds you are using on the backing track

- Avoid copying what you are playing in the exam on the backing track – it should support, not duplicate

- Do you need to include a click track at the beginning?

COPYRIGHT IN A SONG

If you are a singer, instrumentalist or songwriter it is important to know about copyright. When someone writes a song they automatically own the copyright (sometimes called 'the rights'). Copyright begins once a piece of music has been documented or recorded (eg by video, CD or score notation) and protects the interests of the creators. This means that others cannot copy it, sell it, make it available online or record it without the owner's permission or the appropriate licence.

COVER VERSIONS

- When an artist creates a new version of a song it is called a 'cover version'

- The majority of songwriters subscribe to licensing agencies, also known as 'collecting societies'. When a songwriter is a member of such an agency, the performing rights to their material are transferred to the agency (this includes cover versions of their songs)

- The agency works on the writer's behalf by issuing licences to performance venues, who report what songs have been played, which in turn means that the songwriter will receive a payment for any songs used

- You can create a cover version of a song and use it in an exam without needing a licence

There are different rules for broadcasting (eg TV, radio, internet), selling or copying (pressing CDs, DVDs etc), and for printed material, and the appropriate licences should be sought out.

YOUR
PAGE
NOTES